From the Mind of A Servant

A.A GARAY

WESTBOW
PRESS®
A DIVISION OF THOMAS NELSON
& ZONDERVAN

WestBow Press books may be ordered through booksellers or by contacting:

WestBow Press
A Division of Thomas Nelson & Zondervan
1663 Liberty Drive
Bloomington, IN 47403
www.westbowpress.com
844-714-3454

Scriptures are taken from the Holy Bible, New International Version®.
NIV®. Copyright © 1973, 1978, 1984 by International Bible Society.
Used by permission of Zondervan. All rights reserved.

Scriptures are taken from the New King James Version®. Copyright ©
1982 by Thomas Nelson. Used by permission. All rights reserved.

ISBN: 978-1-6642-8561-3 (sc)
ISBN: 978-1-6642-8560-6 (e)

Print information available on the last page.

WestBow Press rev. date: 12/12/2022

This book is dedicated to my parents, Jose Antonio and Carmen Garay; and my older brother, Jose A. Garay Jr. aka "Chue", I love and miss you!

Acknowledgement

And the Journey Continues... Dear lord, it has been a long seven years. As I sit here, at the verge of overcoming my greatest and most difficult challenge, I cannot thank you enough for all that you have rescued me from and are saving me of. Words cannot express the gratitude I have for you. With that said, I want to take this moment to also thank everyone who has taken part in the process of my restoration. My dear Woman/Wife, Tanisha E. Garay. You have been my greatest inspiration; my "Ride or Die"; my best friend and ultimate partner. Unique in every way; a grinder; and fighter (relentless in every way). Loving, genuine, determined to make it work. I love and appreciate all that you have done and continue to do for me.

To my Family, too many to mention. But truly thank you all and I love you all. To my mother in-law, Lady (Sandra Quinones). If you never utter the words, I love you, it will not matter, because you have more than proven your love to me. I love you dearly Lady! Once again, thank you all for your support. Stay blessed!

Contents

1. Struggling to Get Through

On days when you're struggling to get through, we must continue to activate our faith and be reluctant in pursuing our dreams and goals. It's never easy, yet not impossible. Seeing the brightness of the morning motivates me to know that our Redeemer, Jesus is still with us and will help us overcome every obstacle that comes our way. People of God! The Journey continues, hold on! Stay blessed🙏

2. Staying Persistent

Hebrews 12:1-3, "Let us lay aside every weight and the sin which so easily ensnares us and let us run with endurance the race that is set before us". I've Had It! Is our general response when a relationship, job or the like becomes so stressful and overwhelming that we don't think we can continue. Sometimes we can express these words to God when we feel His demands seem overwhelming; or the hurdle's too high to climb; and the obstacles extremely difficult to overcome. Excerpt: Many times, we may get the urgency to want to give in to disappointments. We focus on our situations rather than placing our trust in our Lord God. Even in discouraging times, we must take hold of our faith and put it in action. Let's stay persistent, disregarding the constant attacks of the enemy and pressing through as we seek to reach our highest destination, ETERNAL LIFE in Christ JESUS. Stay blessed! 🙏

3. Confronting Guilt and Shame

Genesis 3:9, "Then the Lord God called to Adam and said to him, where are you?" How do we handle guilt and shame? We have all fallen victim to wanting to disregard the many bad decisions we have made. We try our best to sweep them under the rug, like Adam and Eve did in the Garden of Eden, when they disobeyed God. Unfortunately, the eyes of the lord are too wide and too bright to hide from. We may attempt to use Adam and Eve's deception to justify and silence our own guilt and shame. Nevertheless, our first response should not be to cover our sin, but to accept conviction; confess and genuinely repent to God. Excerpt: Many times, we refuse to take personal responsibility for the things we do and try putting the blame on others. We are each responsible for our actions and decisions. Let's continue to confront our guilt and shame with honesty and sincerity; giving room for our Lord and Savior to restore and clean us of all unrighteousness. Stay blessed! 🙏

4. Standing at the Crossroad

So much has transpire, yet, so much to do. Standing at this crossroad, but I must keep pushing through. The challenges of uncertainties will try to bring despair, but the determination to reach my destiny says keep fighting, you're almost there! As I scan through the pages of this challenging life, I can always look to you, you're my guiding light! When I reminisce on past endeavors, it's sometimes hard to believe, that the man who once was lost, is no longer Me. I'm Overwhelmed; filled with passion; humbled by Grace; standing at this Crossroad committed by Faith. People of God, always remember, when at first you don't Succeed, Keep Striving! Stay blessed! 🙏

5 Just to be Accepted

In this dark lonely world filled with grief and despair, surrounded by evil and no one who cares. Deprived of sincerity and filled with such pain, just to be accepted, the agony still remains. I seek for solutions, I strive to do my best, yet fear and insecurities do not let me rest. And just when I thought there was no way out, I looked to your scriptures and then I can shout, thank God I'm accepted, there is no doubt! People of God! Society and culture many times require high expectations from us. One's that are unrealistic and present illusional goals and dreams. But always remember, we have a realistic God that can provide real results. Just to be accepted, requires one thing, total surrender to our Lord and Mighty King! Stay blessed! 🙏

6. I will no longer hide under a rock

Psalm 27:1 – "The Lord is my light and my salvation; Whom shall, I fear? The Lord is the strength of my life; Of whom shall I be afraid?" (NIV) . Sin has the tendency to leave false guilt in its wake. This can easily push us to a place of isolation, bitterness, and remorse. Some sins wreak havoc on our life as the consequences are played out. We will have to deal with whatever fallout our wrong choices bring, however, we don't have to live the rest of our lives Hiding under a Rock. Fortunately, through the promises of Gods' word we can rest and know that no sin is too great for God to forgive. And when there are repercussions, we don't have to face them alone. I will no longer hide under a rock! People of God always remember, when the going gets tuff the faithful keep praying. Stay blessed! 🙏

7. Flatlined but Mercy said Otherwise

Ephesians 2:1, 4 & 5 - "v1 And you who were dead in trespasses and Sins, v4 But God, who is rich in Mercy, because of his great Love with which He Loved us, v5 Even when we were dead in trespasses, made us Alive together with Christ". The journey of life can many times present unexpected twists and turns. Some that lead us to a path that was never paved nor intended for us to walk. Misdirection and turmoil, I'm gasping for air, about to flatline but mercy said otherwise, hold on, I'm already there. God's rich Mercy, Great Love, and Amazing Grace has pulled me from despair. People of God, Let's keep in mind that we as Christians have been granted "New Life" in this current age and even now share in Christ's Authority. Therefore, we must continue to persevere, even when confronted with adverse situations and tragedies. When death is Crouching at our door, always remember, God has given us New Life through his Love, Blood and Mercy. Stay Blessed! 🙏

8. It's the Past! Let it Go!

Philippians 4:13,14 "Brethren, I do not count myself to have apprehended; but one thing I do, forgetting those things which are behind and reaching forward to those things which are ahead, I press toward the goal for the prize (Eternal life) of the upward call of God in Christ Jesus". We as Christians can sometimes get caught up in our past. Paralyzed and stranded by the bad decisions we have made. Many times because we allow taunts, obstacles, and the outside crowd to deter (side tract) us. It is then that we must learn the valuable benefits of discipline. We must train our mind to strive for the ultimate goal of Salvation; Develop the habit of forgetting what was behind. Not entertain criticism nor ridicule from our past. Maintain our heart on intensely pursuing the calling of the Christian life until Victory has been won. People of God! Dealing with my past has many times placed roadblocks and disappointments in my life. The daily grind of guilt and remorse has sometimes weighed on me, bombarding me with insecurities, discouragement, and doubt. However, I'm learning to push forward knowing that no one is immune to trials, tribulations nor bad decisions. When the enemy (Devil) tries to bring up your past, please remind him of his future! Stay blessed! 🙏

9. P.U.S.H.

P-push, U-until, S-something, H-happens. I'm overwhelmed, exhausted and drained. Trying to patch together the crisis of this lonely world. I seek for answers and resolutions, but I'm met with more stress. I'm speechless, I'm scared, wishing someone was here. I turn, I twist but to no avail, and wonder if somehow, I will prevail. The constant aggression which shades me from light, that wants me to fail without putting up a fight. When the dust settles, the inner Warrior continues to Push and Pull, Toiling my way through thorns and thistles, Hills and Valleys, Hits and misses, disappointments, and fear. Breathing in, breathing out. Using up the last bit of Energy I can mustard. People of God, tragedy has struck the inner core of so many loved ones dearly to our hearts. Many are searching for answers and solutions. Some turning to uncharted territory: Drugs, Violence and Suicide. But, in the midst of all this turmoil and grief, there is "Hope", a wounded healer, JESUS Christ, My Lord and Savior. Will you be willing to give him a try? Stay blessed! 🙏

10. I Am with You

When I fall you catch me, when I'm down you lift me, when I'm hurt you comfort me, when I'm not sure you reassure me, when I'm off track you redirect me, when I'm in desperate need of encouragement your Word (Bible) sustains me. When I look around to find companionship, there you are embracing me. When all seems dark and so far, apart, there is your light shining upon me. When the road to peace and happiness seems so distant, your book of promises tells me different. And when all of life's challenges bombard me with uncertainties, there you are reminding me, son, I am with you till the end of days. The Daily Grind of Life can many times push us to uncharted waters. It is then that we, as property of Christ, shall put our Faith in action and believe that our Lord Jesus will get us through. People of God don't worry, God is already there. Stay blessed!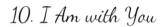

11. "Faith Muscle Prayer"

Heavenly father, as I walk through this maze of Life, I can't always see what's around the corner. I'm not sure what to expect after I take my next step. I need you to strengthen my faith in small ways so I can learn to step out in even bigger ways. Please give me the boldness and courage to exercise my faith muscles and persevere through life's challenging moments. This I pray, Amen. 🙏

12. Lean on God

It is often in the most difficult situations that we feel as though God is not there. The uncertainties and constant torment of life's struggles tend to want our Faith to waver and place us in a mood of discouragement and unbelief. So much, that it feels like God is the furthest from us when he is the closest, he'll ever be. People of God, God may be silent, but he is not still. He will never leave or forsake us. We must learn to trust in the Lord, even when it doesn't make sense. When we choose to lean on God, not only will it bring us comfort and strength, but it will also provide a way to stabilize and reassure our faith. Stay blessed 🙏

13. Good, Good Father

Sometimes our circumstances can be so difficult that we tend to forget how good and dependable God has been to us. We can easily become distracted when we disengage from our priorities. We lay our guards down when we allow superficial things, that carry no substance or value, to rock our foundation. Self-dependence can many times blind us from acknowledging our need for supernatural provision. It is extremely important to pause periodically and look back over our life and see how our great father has guided, guarded, and provided for us along the way. People of God, always remember He is a Good, Good Father, that is who He is! Stay blessed 🙏

14. Fear Not!, Never Alone

Psalm 23:4- "Even though I walk through the Valley of the shadow of death, I fear no evil, for You are with me; Your rod and your staff, they comfort me." Until we are in trying times, we really don't know where our faith stands. Sometimes God allows troubles or trials in our life to get our focus back on Him and the purpose He has for us. We can many times get caught up in a whirlwind of struggles and disappointments, some that can cause us to waver in our faith and allow doubt to crouch at our door. However, we have the ability to cast our eyes on Jesus (the solution) and not on our current circumstances. I cannot promise you that life won't be without winds or health scares. But, when we place our total trust in the lord, we will never have to walk this road alone. God will meet us where we are. We have no need to fear, he is always near, we are Never Alone. Stay blessed🙏

15. Even when

Even when my days seem weary and filled with dismay, I can call out to Jesus and know I'm okay. Even when Loneliness overwhelms me with doubt, I can open my Bible, there's no better rout. And when I feel down with no one to share, even then I hold fast to my Savior's Care. Excerpt: Many times, when faced with adverse situations, we can easily be ensnared by discouraging thoughts, feelings of rejection and even neglect. As I channel through my thoughts, I sometimes loose myself in a ball of emotions that can create periods of isolation and despair. Nevertheless, my ultimate goal, as a Servant of God, is that of someone who is obedient to His calling (nurtured by His word (BIBLE), led by His Holy Spirit) to win and impact souls for His Kingdom. That is my greatest satisfaction, an Eternal life with Jesus will be my greatest reward. Stay blessed🙏

16. Faithful, Faithful You Are

Many times we are tempted to believe that God has promised to keep us from trials, tests, and pain, but when He doesn't, we are disappointed, discouraged, or defeated. However, God has never promised to intercept all things. On the contrary, Jesus said, "I have told you these things, so that in me you may have peace. In this world you will have trouble. But take heart! I have overcome the world (John 16:33, NIV)." Although we will encounter difficult trials it is important to recognize that we must take God at his word and allow him to demonstrate his faithfulness in our time of need. When faced with adverse situations, call on the name of the Lord for direction, wisdom and strength. People of God, we will receive the benefits and blessings that come because of our deep and meaningful relationship with Jesus Christ. And so, we pray, Thank You Heavenly Father for being with us in all these things and giving us the strength to persevere in challenging times and the courage to stand and uphold your mighty Name. Thank You that we need not to fear, doubt, nor worry, because the God who holds the Universe in place holds us together as well. Therefore, we can trust, in our hearts, that Faithful, Faithful you are and always will be. In Your Name we pray, Amen.

17. Rising above our circumstances

Isaiah 60:1, "Arise, shine; For your light has come! And the glory of the Lord is risen upon you." While the pessimist sees the glass half empty, the optimist sees it half full. Many times, our lives can be filled with so much frustration and pain, that even when hope is staring us right in the face, we cannot fathom its possibilities. The world around us can be so cold and cruel. But no matter what the world may throw at us, Jesus has paved the path for us to walk in victory. We need only seek his Kingdom and Righteousness and all else shall fall into place. Excerpt: we can either concede to defeat or allow God to guide our way into victory. It's easy to say we choose Victory, however, are we willing, committed, and dedicated to put our faith in action and rise above our circumstances. Stay blessed🙏

18. Promises

Failure is not an option and fear is false perception. When challenges are coming at you like wildfires in the wilderness, do not be relentless to seek new directions. When the clouds of smoke obstruct your air ways, scratch, and pull, there must be some lead way.

The torrential rainstorms and adversity of daily living may present many obstacles. Those that want to disengage us from staying focus and pursuing our ultimate goals and achievements. When the storms of life impair our vision, we must choose to grab on to the promises of God and move forward with the plans he has designed for us. People of God, regardless of the opposition, we must continue to trust, wait, and lean on the promises of our Lord! Stay blessed 🙏

19. Finding fulfillment for an Empty Life

John 4:3,14 – "Jesus answered and said to her, whoever drinks of this water will thirst again, but whoever drinks of the water that I shall give him will never thirst. But the water that I shall give him will become in him a fountain of water springing up into everlasting life". We can many times go through periods of uncertainties. Regardless of our age or background, feelings of emptiness, loneliness, and despair can easily weigh in on us. It almost feels as if life has become less meaningful and interesting. We can relate with the Samaritan woman at the well when we go through moments of wanting to be loved and accepted. Desperately seeking to satisfy and fill that void in our lives. However, we can only find fulfillment and satisfaction, when we truly and totally surrender our all to the Lord, Jesus Christ. Excerpt: when we place our trust in God and acknowledge that He alone can do what no one else can, He will then fill the void that we've been longing for and complete the plans and blessings that were intended for us to enjoy. Stay blessed 🙏

20. Created for Purpose

Psalm 139:14 – "I will give thanks to You, for I am fearfully and wonderfully made; Wonderful are Your works, and my soul knows it very well". Many times, we can get caught up in the circumstances of life. Things can get overwhelming, and we can easily lose hope. However, if we keep our eyes fixed on the Lord rather than our circumstances, we will gradually begin to see changes. We tend to lose hope when we can't visualize a future. Yesterday was bleak, today is still weary and tomorrow does not seem promising. Fortunately, we as the people of God must always remember, that He who began a good work in us will also complete it (Philippians 1:6). Excerpt: Our life may hold some surprises, but, as long as we know who holds our life, we need not to worry. Stay blessed 🙏

21. May the Lord Find us Ready

Matthew 25:34- "Then the king will say to those on His right hand, come, you blessed of my Father. Inherit the kingdom prepared for you from the foundation of the world". God the father planned to bless His children by including them in the inheritance of His son, which also includes the Glorious kingdom to come, Eternal life. As the children of God, we are confronted with various obstacles and roadblocks. Some to build our character, while others are designed to refine us, in preparation of entering His Glory. It may feel, at times, as if we are being pushed to the brink of folding or giving up. However, we must brace ourselves and hold on to the promises of God to prevail. Regardless of the turmoil, we must endure, staying ready and waiting confidently for the coming of our Lord and Savior, Jesus Christ. Stay blessed🙏

22. Have we switched our focus?

Matthew 14:30- "But when he saw that the wind was boisterous, he (Peter) was afraid; and beginning to sink he cried out, saying, "Lord, save me!" Many times, we as believers experience fearful circumstances because we tend to prioritize things of temporary value, rather than those Eternal. And when we are hit by the storms of life we panic and seek for a way out. It is imperative to evaluate our heart and ask ourselves, have we switched our focus? Whenever we divert our eyes from Jesus, in the midst of our trials and tribulations, our circumstances assume prominence and we lose heart and begin to sink. Nevertheless, we must never lose hope and realign our heart and mind to God's word. A key truth to reset our situation is to know that "The difference between fear and faith is focus" (Dr. David Jeremiah). People of God lets continue to prioritize eternal values and not allow fear and uncertainties to hinder the ultimate prize that our Heavenly Father has set aside for us. Stay blessed🙏

23. Following God's Schedule

Romans 11:36- "For of Him and through Him and to Him are all things, to whom be glory forever. Amen". We enjoy the benefits of feeling in control of our own schedule, and many times it can be frustrating when things don't go according to plan. Consider how we pray about concerning situations in our life. Without realizing it, we may be demanding that the Lord follow the schedule we've constructed based on our very limited human wisdom and understanding. Yet, if we believe God is who He says He is, how can surrendering to His way not be to our benefit? Excerpt: unlike us, the Lord has complete knowledge about our life - past, present, and future. He understands our every motive and anticipates our every move. When we find ourselves wanting to do things our way, we not only delay the process to receive God's blessing in our lives, but we also create unwanted stress and discomfort. We can enjoy the goodness of God's heart by allowing him to guide us and manifest his powerful plan and purpose in our lives. By following God's Schedule, we can ultimately experience the joy and peace of His Glory. Stay blessed🙏

24. Overcoming Fear with Truth

John 8:32- "And you shall know the truth, and the truth shall make you free" (NKJV). Fear and Anxiety can enslave us and shift our perspective to the point that we live in a constant state of confusion and unease. But we as the People of God must recognize that we have a heavenly Father who has promised to take care of us. We must identify the root cause of our fears. It's easy to recognize surface causes, but ultimately, the root of our apprehension is a distrust of God. We must learn how to focus on the Lord instead of our Fears. When negative thoughts and emotions enter our hearts, we can overcome them with the Word of Truth, the Bible. God has a bag of goodies, always at our disposal, that speak truth to every situation: Greater is He that is in me, than he that is in the world (1 John 4:4); Even though I walk through the valley of the shadow of death, I will fear no evil (Psalm 23:4); Fear not, I am with you. I am your God. I will strengthen and help you (Isaiah 41:10). Footprints – when we feel that we're walking this journey alone, He was carrying us all along. People of God, in times of trouble, meditating on the Word of God and holding fast to its' truth is a powerful and effective tool, which can help us overcome fear. Stay blessed🙏

25. Surviving Life's Storms

Mark 4:39 – "Then He arose and rebuked the wind, and said to the sea," Peace, be still! And the wind ceased and there was a great calm". In all of life's storms, we must remember that Jesus is present; He is sovereign, and nothing comes as a surprise to Him. God will never leave nor forsake us. If we know this, we can trust that He will bring peace into every situation that we encounter. No matter how strong the winds blow, and the sea of problems rise up in our daily lives, let's grab hold of our ultimate anchor, Jesus Christ and rest assured that He will always land us safely at His intended destination. Stay blessed 🙏

26. Prayer, Our Lethal Weapon

Prayer is our most powerful tool for shaping the world around us. When we give time, attention, and priority to conversations with our Father there are no limits to what He can achieve through and for us. It is through our interactions with people that we can see the effectiveness of prayer and the results of its power. Prayer, in many ways, can bring clarity, provide healing, and guide us into all of Gods truth and purpose. "For the weapons of our warfare are not carnal, but mighty through God to the pulling down of strongholds" (2 Corinthians 10:4). Prayer can be used as our lethal weapon against the attacks and schemes of the enemy and life. "The effectual fervent prayer of a righteous man availeth much" (James 5:16 KJV). People of God, let prayer (the open channel of communication with God) continue to flow in our everyday life. In stressful situations we can easily lose track of the power of prayer. As we continue our daily journey, we must actively pursue to make time and utilize the lethal weapon God has placed in our hands, Prayer. 1 Thessalonians 5:17- "pray without ceasing". Stay blessed 🙏

27. We Would Rather Pray

Psalm 109:4- "In return for my love they are my accusers, but I give myself to prayer". When someone betrays us or turns against us, we can easily lose control and want to seek revenge. Nevertheless, we must turn over our anger and frustration to the Lord and seek His face in prayer. It can be extremely difficult to overcome hurt and disappointment, especially after we've demonstrated a genuine act of love and kindness. Fortunately, we have a heavenly Father who can sympathize and empathize with all we encounter. He knows how to best deal with the situation and guide us into making wise Christlike decisions. We just need to lend our ears to His voice and the prompting of His Holy Spirit. Stay blessed 🙏

28. The Straw that Stirs our Soul

Isaiah 48:17- "I am the Lord your God. Who teaches you what is best for you". Taking the Road most travel can feel beneficial and accommodating. We are obsessed with the need for speed and prefer to microwave our way to accomplish the things we desire. Unfortunately, this approach can lead us into making unwise decisions that may cause catastrophic consequences. Loss of freedom, relationships and ultimately death. However, when we allow our Lord and Savior, Jesus Christ to be The Straw that Stirs our Soul, it can completely change the outlook of our future. Placing our complete trust in the Lord may not always be easy, but always rewarding. Although God may allow us to confront difficult situations and extremely tight circumstances, we can rest to know that our dear father will do it for our very best and is stirring us to produce the finest outcome. "If He leads us to it, He will lead us through it!" People of God, will we let the Lord be The Straw that Stirs our Soul? Stay blessed 🙏

29. An Attitude of Gratitude

Sometimes when I'm going through the mundane of days I can look up and see the wonderful works of your hands and the beauty that surrounds your creation. Even when I don't feel it, I know you are with me, and when my heart wants to deceive me, I lean on your promises. Through it all I've decided to rest in you and develop an Attitude of Gratitude for all you have done, and all you will do. People of God, "the greater the level, the bigger the devil." Let's continue to activate our faith and push through even when adversity tells us otherwise. Stay blessed 🙏

30. Incarcerated (lest we forget)

Matthew 25:36 "...I was in prison, and you came to visit me"; Hebrews 13:3 "Remember the prisoners as if chained with them - those who are mistreated-since you yourselves are in the body also." There is no greater challenge than when your freedom has been compromised. My prison experience has been, by far, my greatest obstacle to overcome. The constant hostility and endless oppression can lead you down a road of hopelessness and self-destruction. Unfortunately, the outside world can easily lose tract of those who are suffering the consequences of their bad decisions. "Out of sight, out of mind", can best be described for those who have not been through or faced with this terrible ordeal. Nevertheless, we as the People of God should not lose sight of the severity and need of those that have been labeled and outcast. We must Remember and do our best to Pray and demonstrate God's Love to them. This can be done by writing letters of encouragement, mailing inspirational materials, and blessing them with care packages. Lest we forget! it's required by the word of God! (The Bible). Stay blessed 🙏

Printed in the United States
by Baker & Taylor Publisher Services